14

This book belongs to:

Larson

BIG & EASY™

Indians

A LEARN TO READ BOOK

By Donald Silver
Illustrated by Patricia J. Wynne

CHECKERBOARD PRESS
NEW YORK

ISBN 002-898255-X Printed in U.S.A. Library of Congress Catalog Card Number: 89-637

0 9 8 7 6 5 4 3 2 1

The first Americans were Indians.

They hunted with spears.

Some Indians lived in wigwams.

Wigwams were made of bark and poles.

Some Indians lived in teepees.

A teepee is a tent.

There were Indians who lived on cliffs.

They were farmers.

Plains Indians hunted buffalo.

They ate the meat and used the skin.

Cheyenne
Great Plains

Many Indians fished in rivers.

They also grew corn.

Some Indians hunted whales in canoes.

These Indians carved totem poles, too.

At special times Indians wore masks.

They danced and played games.

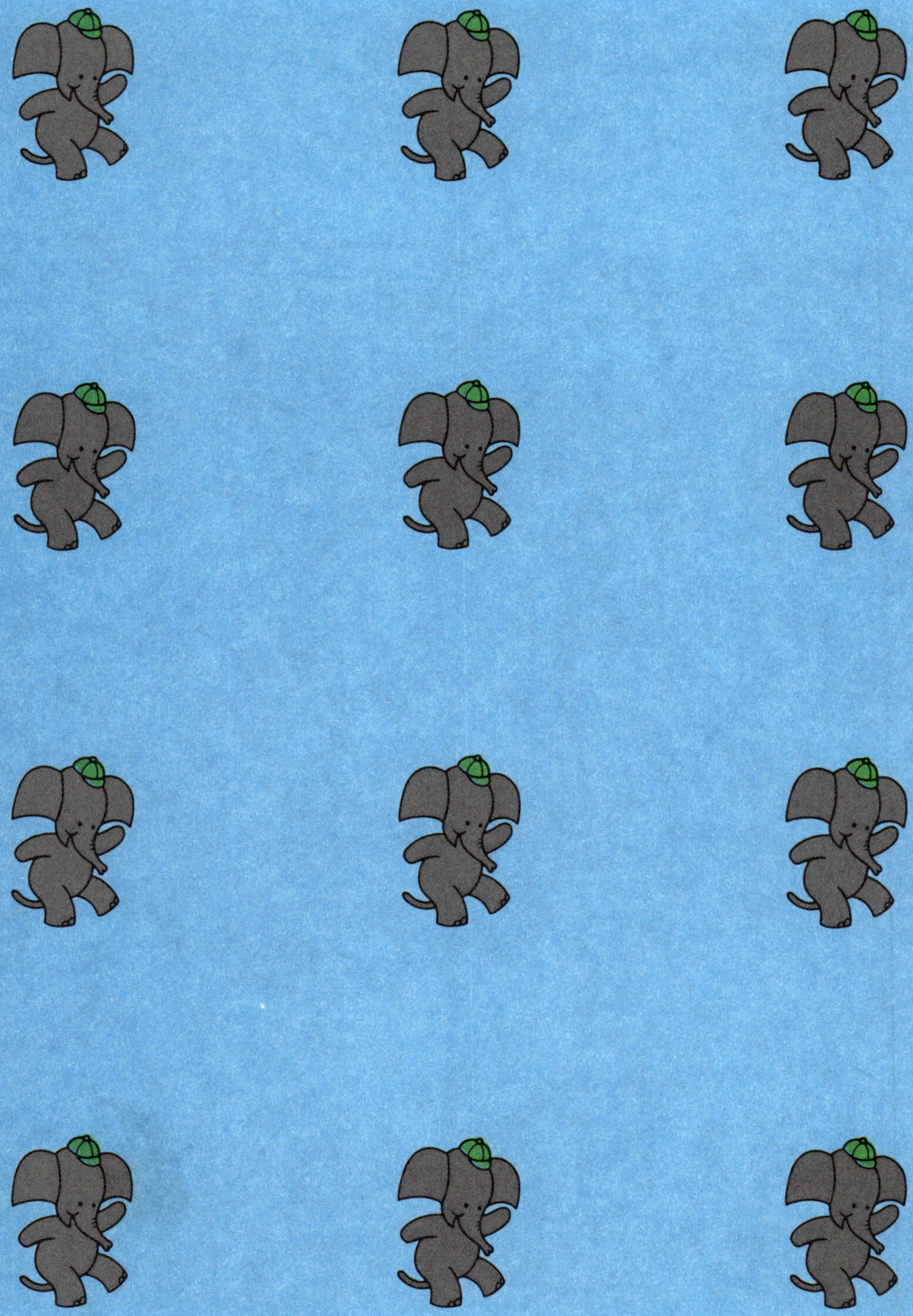